# PRESS DIONYSUS
## 2021

First published in 2021 by PRESS DIONYSUS LTD in the UK, 167, Portland Road, N15 4SZ, London.

www.pressdionysus.com

Paperback

ISBN: 978-1-913961-06-0

# Walking with Camels

## *A CURE FOR MADNESS*

## Tony Howson

**PRESS DIONYSUS**

Press Dionysus •
ISBN- 978-1-913961-06-0
© 2021 Press Dionysus
First Edition, September 2021, London

•All images contained in the book are owned by the author.

Editor: Ege Tuvay
Cover art: Zeynep Özatalay - S.Deniz Akıncı

Press Dionysus LTD, 167, Portland Road, N15 4SZ,
London
• e-mail: info@pressdionysus.com
• web: www.pressdionysus.com

## About the Author

Tony Howson was born in Slough, UK, on November 14, 1956. Since then, he has lived in 30 different homes around the world and experienced a life of storytelling. He currently lives in Turkey with his wife and daughter. Tony also has three sons and two grandchildren. He worked as a journalist in broadcast and print, but for 25 years has been active in international development, training journalists in Africa, Middle East, former Soviet Union and Asia to make programmes that empower local people and support media development. He has an honorary doctorate for services to journalism from Uzhgorod University in Ukraine. Outside of journalism he has delivered poetry readings and storytelling sessions and courses to help others develop their techniques. He has had a previous collection of poems and essays published, and had work included in anthologies. He has also had three photo exhibitions, held in the UK and Ukraine. One exhibition supported a production of his four-voice performance piece, "SHUSH!", performed in Scarborough, one of his favourite home towns. His formative years were spent on Teesside, once known for its steel and chemical industries. He went on to report its decline in the 1980s. He has also contributed to community arts, helping to set up Scarborough Flair, a project leading to a series of productions, based around the spoken word. Other activities included supporting mental health organisations and establishing a pioneering victim-offender mediation project in Sheffield.

## About the Book

To survive a mad world you need camels. They are like the Praetorian Guard. Walk with them and they act like a shield-wall, guarding your space so you can try and make sense of what is going on. This book of poetry, prose and pictures allows you to eavesdrop on a personal global trek through the minefields of madness, reflecting on events past, present and future. It starts with a gun to the head, weaves around global trouble-spots and embraces love lost and gained. Treading in camel footprints, you cross continents in search of that elusive cure for insanity.

## Comments and reviews on Walking with Camels

"A lifetime of remote and often dangerous travel is distilled in this remarkable collection of experience and thought. The poems, photographs and narrative shine a light into some troubled corners of the world in a profound, moving and deeply personal way."

**Nick Adcock – Journalism trainer**


"How glad I am to see the poems 'The playground', 'Easter 1993/2015', 'When Slavic brothers meet', 'Sehnsucht', 'The women's conference...Somalia' and 'Istanbul' in this book."

**Felix Hodcroft - Poet**


"Rarely has contemporary poetry impacted so personally on me. Howson has known murderously bumpy places, uncertain times and the addictive nature of risk. Behind his eyes are images that do not fade and, in his head, wisdom that doesn't give way to cynicism. Instead, they imbue his verse and prose with a reporter's awareness of truths - political and human - that his trade cannot always adequately reflect."

**Geoffrey Seed**
**Author and former investigative journalist**


"I'm tempted to say that it's sui generis. The form as well as the story is uniquely Howson. The only reference I have is with some of the books of John Berger."

**Christopher Hale**
**Non-fiction writer and documentary producer**

"When I came to the end, I felt really quite emotional! I like the prose pieces which add interest and context and give a bit of a break from the emotional intensity of the poetry which is really great! There is variety in style appropriate to the subject matter...beautifully illustrated for me in 'Istanbul' but equally present in most of the work. Lovely."

**Jane Sudworth - Writer**

"This is lyrical thinking from the writer's 'nomadic hopscotch existence', a rewarding journey of words through landscapes, politics and feelings. Here is a man who has stared into the flames, from Somalia to Istanbul, but is also not afraid to talk about the soul or to celebrate a spicy meal with friends. He writes, sometimes elliptically in poetry and sometimes pointedly in prose, of things that seem to be always with us – concentration camps, prisons, rigged elections, sunrises and sunsets, sorrow, dancing and love. I invite you to walk with him in the camels' footsteps. By the end of your journey, you will have learned some wisdom about the strange, unjust and often beautiful world we live in, and you will have made a new friend."

**Adam Strickson**
**Writer and theatre director working at the University of Leeds**

"It`s one of the most mesmerizing things I have read. In a word, brilliant. It`s a clever, fascinating theme that works, and the intertwining of a vast range of human emotions and experiences holds the reader to the page. A masterstroke."

**Beranice Semp- Journalist (retired)**

*This book is dedicated to my wife, Rengin and daughter Maya. Also to my three sons, Oli, Tom and Denis; daughters-in-law Anna and Jane, and granddaughters Ella Rose and Josie. Thank you guys.*

**Walking with Camels: Step Back**

To cure madness, you need to step into madness. To walk camels through a climate that is hot, hell and humid implies a certain insanity. The landscape is semi-arid, sun-baked hard ground with near invisible trails carved into it. Bushes spiked with long, sharp needles, cling to the ground around the tracks. Between the branches stretch large webs, with giant spiders waiting for their prey.

Within this landscape I find my camels. To reach them, I once hitched a ride on the bed of a converted pick-up truck that had been used as a Technical, a war-vehicle designed to carry a mounted machine gun. Balanced on the back, we went charging through those sticky spider webs. I spent most of the journey un-sticking my hair, face and arms from the clinging protein some call silk.

Another time I rode on a "qat" or "khat" lorry heading back through the Ogaden Desert after delivering its precious cargo. This was a high-speed journey made treacherous by a driver who continuously chewed the qat, which looks like the leafy branches of a privet hedge and acts like amphetamine. The easiest was a four-wheel drive, where I got to steer and bump through this challenging terrain.

My camels, to the best of my knowledge, are still in Somalia, being cared for by a generous nomad. When I visited, I branded the calves that were designated mine. I estimate that I have at least eight camels. But who knows? Over time it is hard to stay in touch with a nomadic camel herder, especially when the chances to visit became less and less as life moves on. Somalia has faced many crises over livestock disease and environmental issues creating a shortage of grazing areas, as well as the left-overs from past conflict. This means herders and camels risk stepping into mined areas to find food.

It is around 30 years since I bought my first camel in Somalia. During that time these beasts have been burdened by disease, hunger, violent tensions and me. Somalia and Somaliland, the northern state that has no official recognition, are firmly embedded in what I call the Band of Tragedy, sandwiched between the Tropic of Cancer and the Tropic of Capricorn. I have visited many of the countries within this band, as well as those on it fringes. Start with Somalia. It is hard to pinpoint when suffering started, but the Ogaden War in 1977 could be a marker. Conflict continued from that point, through the civil war that ended in 1991, and in-fighting continues. Fighting always leaves a long-term legacy. In the case of Somalia, one of the lasting leftovers has been landmines.

Human Rights Watch reported in 2020 ongoing armed conflict, insecurity, lack of state protection, and recurring humanitarian crises "exposed Somali civilians to serious abuse. There are an estimated 2.6 million internally displaced people, many living unassisted and vulnerable to abuse."

Trace a line and see war torn Syria and Yemen. In Gaza, West Bank and Israel, hard-headedness has turned that region into an unholy land. Head to India and Covid 19 chaos will leave its historic scar. A fifth of the way into the 21st Century and conflict-ridden Myanmar's death toll rises. Go the other way and see the devastation of West Africa, shattered by conflict followed by deep poverty, to be kicked again by the Ebola crisis. Wars may stop but the tragic consequences roll forward.

Poverty is the umbrella term and excuse for the tragedy. Here is a parsimonious explanation I came across of what poverty is. It includes poor health, unsafe drinking water, and lack of education, personal safety, and human rights. What really defines poverty concerns the ability of families to have enough food and resources to survive on a day-to-day basis.

The World Bank estimates that by 2030, up to two-thirds of the world's extreme poor will live in "countries characterised by fragility, conflict and violence."

I live far from poverty. But its existence does impact on how I feel about life. I walk camels to cope.

Walking my camels, taking them on journeys looking for food, camping under the stars, drinking strong coffee with Somali nomads, and swapping stories, smoking strong cigarettes, chewing qat, all that romance is now played out in my head. Walking my camels in the unstable state of my head, is my cure for madness. I move them around the canyons of my mind. As we walk, I try to make sense of experiences because they impact on how I see and feel about myself and the world I live in. I do not visit places of extreme hardship to stand, to stare. I go because it is where work has often taken me. I have shrugged off many bad names in my time, but I would detest being called a poverty tourist, or a war tourist. In fact, I would detest just to being labelled a tourist. Come walk with me. Wear good shoes, the journey can twist and turn and roads may be rocky.

Along the way you will meet Egal, a young boy I photographed when visiting his dad's house in Somaliland. As the women ate inside, we, about six men, sat in the yard eating spaghetti, goat meat, rice. Egal, then aged four, taught me how to eat spaghetti with my fingers, an art I have not really used since. I was useless at it but certainly made him laugh. I was good at eating rice, cupping it into a hollow in my fist and then pushing it into my mouth with a movement of the thumb. It is good to make a child laugh when around him there had been so much tension. About 30 years on I wonder where Egal is now.

I had this picture of Egal in my study. I had to take it down. His eyes followed me everywhere.

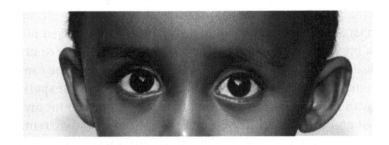

## Egal's Eyes

Your tracking eyes, Egal,
They turn the parchment pages
Back to those Somali days.
We ate greasy goat meat and rice.

You, a reminder of the boy in Sheffield
Who could not paint blue.
All he saw were diving jets,
Strafing.

Out of the blue, a finger snap,
He became a refugee.

I told your father
What I had seen in the hills,
That day I felt useless.

The baby boy's scarred foot.
A mother's scream cut the air
As the ricochet struck.

How does he walk today
On that crippled foot?

Me, crouching behind a rock,
Unable to reach out, useless.
Zing, zing, singing above my head.

The music has never stopped.

Zing, zing, zing. Like
A screeching violin.

Drink the camels' milk, Egal.

As your father told me, hand
Cupping greasy meat and rice,
Eat like a Somali. Tomorrow

You may be hungry or have no need of food.

## Tiger's Feet

Here they are,
Tiger's sandals.

They are very clever.
He was clever.
             A survivor.
He stole a soldier's boots
And, with a hunting knife,
Cut them, shaped them
To be worn
           On either foot.

*Tiger's sandals – placed so he knew where to find them in the dark. When British MP Tony Worthington was kidnapped in Somaliland in 1994, Tiger told me he was involved in the rescue, which apparently took place under a hail of bullets. I have different accounts of this, some exaggerated.*

That is Tiger sly.
He told me why,

You never know when trouble strikes.
He said,
Often it happens in darkness of night.
You may have to run,
               Or stay and fight.
But to do so without your boots on
                Would not be right.

He wore them for years.
Walked miles around the Horn,
Through the original Garden of Eden,

Amongst pin-prick thorns and sharp rocks,
In sinful sunburnt punished desert
Where The Devil lives.

Tiger taught survival tricks.
As we camel-walked that desert,
Amongst those red-rust stones
And parched, shadowless places.
He pointed to the Gulf,
To the holy man's grave,
Near to where the tide turns.
A well of sweet water.
                    Tiger knowledge.

With a pharyngeal laugh,
He said, pick up a rock.
Place money beneath
To appease The Devil.
Ethereal magic at play.
But the vanishing notes,
Dank and crumpled,
Were never used,
So far as I and eyes could see,
                    To buy new shoes.

**Visit to a centre caring for mine victims**

Slalom screams split the darkness,
Echoing off the dull whitewashed walls.
The collective sound ducks through holes in houses
Blasted there by bazookas. Homes
On streets where the land is pushed up.

Skulls and cross-bones, tape fluttering.
You come across them on travels
With camels or on curious walks
And talks about types of mines
That leave you legless,
                or turn you into mist.

I understood the screams, thinking of him
Tied to his bed, a shaking cot. A head
Filled with madness and nightmares.
He wanted to run but had no legs.
Like a fish out of water, unlucky him.
He was not dead.
The mine he stood on did not kill him.
But trapped him, with thirty others,
In the insanity of surviving. Not even
The stars could calm him.

He could not walk with camels.

## Dead Fish

Romantic me, straddling the equator,
Looking at the star-filled universe –
A sky with diamonds north and south.
There was one fish in the market today.
Hungry people stared at it, wide eyed.

A fish, unflappable, dead. It stared back
But could not match the emptiness
Of the human eye.

A fish, netted fresh
From the sea and brought to a land
Of second freshness. A fish
Too precious to eat.

## The Playground

My playground was an old pillbox
Next to a rancid pond we kids
Rafted across. With sticks for guns,
Stones for grenades, we killed each other.
Only to rise again to read Men-Only.
Torn pages found in dens deep in bushes.
We were heroes, our minds scarred
By what it is to be manly. And we knew war.
We had seen the Saturday night films.

Long barrels on wheels.
and look-a-like drainpipes,
All strangely out of place behind wire.
The weapons are coming back in.
The multiple rocket launchers,
The superguns of yesterday,
That once sent deathly rains
Onto the heads of
Whoever's turn it was.

The foot-soldiers are being re-trained
In building skills, or de-mining. But
Kalashnikovs and pistols remain hidden
In unmarked places, beneath earth and sand,
A shovel always close at hand. A bullet
Nearby.

I turn to watch the children play.
They have sticks for guns and stones for grenades.
They chase around the bombed-out homes,
Stick fingers in holes in bullet-riddled walls.
They shout, scream, get up. Drop their sticks.
Kick a can. Argue, scrap and bully. And,
As they grow, their fathers will tell them
Where the guns are buried, to understand
What it is to be a man.

## Easter: Hargeisa 1993/Addis Ababa 2015

A vision salted in sin,
Peppered in memory,
Shimmered on my horizon
As incense and camels guided me to holy caves.

---

It was a black day in Hargeisa.
One that inspires madness.
And deeds of no-regret.
Darkening folds of sky
Lowered to kiss
Red dusty earth

And turn it into mud,
And the mud into rivers
The colour sinners fear.

Deaf to doubt under the rain-rattled tin roof.

Caught alone, we sat, we talked
As war-like roars raged outside
In a world of limited time, of space.

---

Her ghost appeared in Addis Ababa,
At the bus stop when I looked
Through a half-steamed window,
A borderline bodach memory of rains.

That day she travelled with me to those ancient caves of memory
And worship.

We curled within our turned back time,
Beneath our umbrella of confession,
That wheel, those spokes turning
As we turned into each other.

We, like cogs compelling each other
Until the oil dried and the teeth
Fractured and cracked like
The steaming, drying earth.

And she lowered her headscarf, giving it me to hold.

Silk sliding with a sigh.
And, in its smell, I discovered
Her world, her place, her taste.
Our confessions fell as silence,
Like coins into a brimmed hat
We would have to wear again.
Speaking crimes to be stoned for,
Repeating acts we atone for.

As I whispered the guilt of no regret
To the flickering candles and icon of love,
Within the shadow corners of the caves,
She stopped warming my back and sighed,
Her hair woven in the stale air and incense.

---

Yeast smells and sweat, I again
Wear my coat of sins.
Time-faded with blown grit and rain.
The singing,
      The prayer
Grinds to a stop, brakes biting
Addis Ababa, journey's end.

A shadow in a bus window, nothing more.
An Ethiopian woman dressed in blue.
Nothing more but a singular
Move. A turn of head, a look,
To say goodbye, never to look again.
Except in a memory divided by a desert,
Hazy and lingering long after the rains dried,
After she had re-pinned her headscarf.

## Walking with Camels: Sidestep.

During the Somali civil war that ended in 1991, many fled to safety and became refugees, enduring the camps in Kenya, Ethiopia, before many reaching Europe and the United States. They left for a better, more peaceful, and safer life. Some probably found it, others not. There is something hollow about having to run away when you cannot stop loving what is behind you.

Many, after their torturous trek, came to Sheffield. They brought with them their clan rivalries. They were not made overly-welcome. They became rivals within the refugee communities. It was this localised conflict that took me to Somalia and Somaliland. I wanted to find out where these people were from and what they had experienced. I travelled with a Somali called Joharri, who had led around 80 people from the north to safety in Ethiopia. For almost three months, I explored, made stories to share, recorded poets, musicians and learnt about the benefits of camels.

The civil war displaced 1.5 million people. That is a significant number but as years passed, conflicts around the Band of Tragedy saw larger numbers. The 2021 figures showed more than 6.6 million Syrians had been forced to flee their country and another 6.7 million people remained internally displaced. The vast majority – approximately 5.5 million Syrian refugees –found refuge in neighbouring countries, primarily Turkey. For me, this is not a numbers game. It is a political, social and emotional crisis in respecting life.

With the passage of time, roots get left behind, as people drown seeking safety, as people settle away from their heartland. Deep traditions weaken. Generations divide. Old practices fade. Identity becomes a crisis. Notions of acceptance and rejection go to war. Interviewing teenagers in Sheffield many years ago, one Somali told me: "Somali boys are only interested in white girls. They are not interested in Somali girls anymore because they say we don't have a clitoris and cannot enjoy sex. So, they reject us." This was a reference to female genital mutilation, a practice common right across the Band of Tragedy. The practice is inhuman, often approved by parents, but creates another void for people looking for a new life.

One cultural shift came in sport. Somali boys enjoyed running and soccer. But many migrants who went to the United States started to move away from their traditional sporting passions. They discovered American Football.

It can be a brutal game. In the 2011 Bleacher Report into identifying the world's toughest sport, it was sixth. Rugby - that "thugs game played by gentlemen" – was fourth and number one was water polo where underwater activity is quite sly. Playing in a team gave some boys a sense of place and value, but for others it can be a reminder of a violent world.

I discovered this sporting cultural shift amongst migrant and refugee communities as I researched the death of George Perry Floyd Jnr. He was an African American killed by police. A store clerk claimed he had passed a counterfeit

$20 bill in Minneapolis. Derek Chauvin, one of four police officers who arrived on the scene, knelt on Floyd's neck and back for 9 minutes and 29 seconds. Events of that day in May 2020, led to a worldwide protest against racism.

Floyd's death put Minneapolis firmly on the map as a centre for institutional racism. At that time, around 80,000 people of Somali heritage were said to be living in Minneapolis. Figures do vary and lower numbers were also recoded. But it was not just Somalis who found themselves in Minnesota. People came from all over the world, including South America, Asia, Middle East and Africa. In my research I came across Kader, a rising football star studying in one of the state's most racially diverse high schools.

According to the Wall Street Journal, Kader shared a roster with "slender Somali-American kids who had never played a down but wanted to try the nation's most popular high school sport. "

Sixteen-year-old Kader Diop had cycled to the peaceful protest against the killing of Floyd and the institutional racism endemic in the U.S. Thousands of people were walking the Interstate-35W bridge in Minneapolis. Suddenly a tanker truck was heading for the crowd. Kader thought "I was about to die." He leapt out of the way and suffered a scraped knee. No one was injured. The near miss was judged an accident by the authorities.

I also read about Hamza, another rising star. But, with respect to his sporting prowess, I was more interested in his mother, whose story told more about the human stress and pain caused by conflict.

*Fear, Protection and Defiance*

## Kumbaya Hopes

Olive branches dropped,
Trampled under-foot by
Thousands of feet walking,
Some running, crossing the
Bridge that links the divide.

Keep your eyes open.
You've got to know when
To run, to hide, to fly.
You've got to see
When the mood moves
Away from peace.
You have got to see
When the tanker truck comes,
Barrelling toward the crowd,
Shredding kumbaya hopes.

Listen, don't cock the gun,
Cock the ears.
Listen to the crowd.
Listen to the screams and chants,
They wait for the whistle.
Voices:
*He is angry at 46.*
*I am angry at 31.*
*You are angry at 16.*

*You will be angry at 31.*
*I will be angry at 46.*
*He was angry at 16,*
   *And so was I.*

Quick flick hip
Speed turn, away
From the volatile state.

It is Kader's move
Against the engine's stench
And rubbery squeal.
A flesh wound,
A cut knee.

The Tigers Football team
Stayed intact that day.
But who won the game?
When will the final whistle blow

**Blitz** *(In American football, A blitz is when a higher than usual number of defensive players rush the opposing quarterback, in an attempt either to tackle him or force him to hurry his pass attempt).*

Hamza has tears in his eyes
As his brother Kaafi kisses his cheek.
Victory brings delight.
It comes with medals, trophies
Won on the battlefield of play
In a small,
Rural town called Willmar.

Now they want to
Blitz. American style.

Hamza is a rare Somali.
He plays American football.
He's breaking barriers for
Race and acceptance.
"I just want peace," he says.
But the friction is war,
Control is the key,
To force the battlefield blunders,
Take down the leaders,
Hold the ground.
Sneak in the *COINdanistas,*
Bring on the cheer and fear
From the on-lookers cry.

*Hit them hard, hit them low, hit them again.*
Hamza and Kaafi sat in silence
At the dinner table. Their mum,
She wants peace.
Peace, from the lion's roar of planes.
From the three lines of effort:
Defence,
       Offence
           Special teams.
Peace from the unfair fight,
From dominance and tears
That no timeout can dry.
She sells trinkets from her shop.
It is in Willmar, her false home.
She has never seen Hamza play,
Helmeted, uniformed and ready to go.
Violence, always her greatest fear,
Lurking around a corner,
Lurking on the football pitch,
Entering her shop before opening time,
Entering her shop when a bell rings.
The door opens. She serves the customer.
Every time a shadow at the window pauses,
The gun chambers roll roulette style.
How many losers she has known.
Live or die, always an unmarked question.


Her family died in the battlefield blitz.

**Djibouti Airport some years ago**

I am thinking of that day, years ago now,
In Djibouti airport, Somalis waiting for a plane.

I stood listening to young guys talking,
Comparing some latest electronic game.

And the girl who said to her friend: "I don't wanna
Fucking go." And the other agreed: "I wanted to stay
home."

Teenagers dressed for a coffee meet in Sheffield
Flop around and crowd as parents stare with duty.

The father said they must see their homeland,
It is their way of life, their blood, their collective soul.

But there is no McDonalds in Hargeisa, it is camel culture,
And the last time I was there, all the roofs were blown.

*Girl standing on a hillside, watching a stranger with his camels.*

**Walking with Camels: Madness**

*The futility of pushing madness away*

Madness. You cannot push it away. You must embrace it. That is what my mind-walking with camels helps me achieve. My madness started on the Cote D'Ivoire border with Liberia. Cote D'Ivoire was my first African experience. I found myself caught up in the tragedy of Africa without being prepared for any of it. I kept meeting a lot of Roman Catholic priests, mainly frustrated men in cassocks watching their flock die before them. HIV was spreading, people were dying, and the church was saying don't use condoms. In some cases, whole villages were infected. And then there was the war.

I met traumatised priests who had been left numbed and shocked by the killing of five nuns near the Liberian capital of Monrovia. The bodies had been shot, mutilated and left rotting in the sun. This was 1992.

In November, 2018,Reporter Abdi Latif Dahir wrote for QuartzAfrica: "For 14 years, between 1989 and 2003, a brutal civil war ravaged the nation leading to the death of close to 250,000 people. Women were raped and mutilated; warlords recruited child soldiers to fuel the conflict; tens of thousands of people were displaced and fled the country. The full freight of the war, its callousness, and its collateral effect have continued to remain a defining marker of the West African state."

Being so close to the border, meant there was always a risk. I got on a bus from the Ivorian town of Man, heading to its largest city, Abidjan. The bus stopped at a false checkpoint. I was pulled off the bus and made to kneel in mud as an officer with a posh English accent quizzed me. Sometimes calm, sometimes shouting, sometimes trying to be a friend, he wanted to know everything I had seen and been doing. He claimed to have been trained at the leading army school for officers, Sandhurst. As this was going on, a ragged looking soldier, thin, wearing baggy torn clothes, pressed the barrel of his Kalashnikov into my forehead. He made a show of flicking off the safety catch.

To this day I feel I should be dead. I have bad dreams and flashbacks. When I got back to Sheffield, where I lived in a nice, modern detached house, I felt lost and could not fit back into that world of middle-class comfort. I have had other bad experiences, such as a hand-grenade rolling down the corrugated roof of the house I was staying in and four of us staring at each other, hardly breathing, waiting for it to go off. It didn't. During that same trip, I was shot at, caught in cross-fire, saw mass graves being dug up. Since then, I watched a double beheading streamed live in Libya, and met traumatised people who have been caught up in conflict. Many have experiences worse than mine, ranging from rape to being hacked by machetes.

In 2015, as I travelled out of Freetown, Sierra Leone, I met a woman who owned a roadside shop. During the Liberian war, as rebels closed in on Freetown, she was dragged into the road, repeatedly raped, had both arms and legs hacked off and left for dead with warning notices hung around her neck. She survived. She had children. I am reminded traumatised people are not to be called victims, but survivors.

It took some years for me to be diagnosed as having Post Traumatic Stress Disorder, which thanks to the tablets and regular walks with camels, I continue to manage. There is no cure, it is all about management. Up until the point of diagnosis I was a miserable being. Identifying a cause opened a gateway in the mind and let the camels in. I am tired of conflict and the constant worldly reminder of its causes.

In 1996 I moved to Kyiv, Ukraine, and although I continued to travel and stay for long periods in different places, this city of sun-glinting onion domed churches, horse-chestnut trees and cold winters, was my home base until 2013. I found myself constantly faced with corrupt practices and under regular watch by the SBU (formerly KGB). This was largely because of the *Gongadze* affair – a journalist beheaded because of revelations about the President, Leonid Kuchma - and because of work around media freedom and elections. I witnessed the 2004 Orange Revolution and its subsequent betrayal. During the revived protest in 2014 in Kyiv, my son Denis, was working for the Red Cross when he and others came under fire by snipers.

This is how Britannica.com summarised it all as an estimated 25,000 protestors occupied a fortified camp in Kyiv's Maidan, or Independence Square. On February 18, 2014, it announced 20 people killed. Two days later it reports *the Maidan is transformed into a charred battleground, as protesters ignite massive bonfires to stymie attempts by security forces to retake the square. EU leaders agree to level sanctions against those in Ukraine believed to be responsible for the violence.*

*Protestors during the Orange Revolution gather at a political rally in Kyiv, Ukraine. There were big screens so protesters could see protesters... but it remains a question: were the people's voices truly heard?*

## Then Russia annexed Crimea

I had worked with Tatars in Crimea and Russian speakers in the Donbass region, which became the frontline of a numbing conflict that many tried to ignore. This conflict divided families and people with shared histories and political belief, and through it maintained tension between Russia and the NATO alliance. It left Ukraine in a state of flux, adding to its constant identity crisis. Ukraine means, in many translations, borderland. In others, a kind of no-man's land. A hinterland. It has been a pawn on one square of the world's chessboard. It has been surrounded by traitorous kings.

With all this going on around me, it felt good to discover the joy of walking with camels, even if it was limited to the mind. They soothed my madness with a gentle rocking as they walked, their listening skills unique. Sadly, they do little to sooth the madness of the world outside my head.

## Madness

Tonight, shall I write of madness?
Not of the kind found rampant in Bedlam,
But of the madness that infects the sane.

It is the madness that makes them scream,
Arms raised to the moon. To scream again
In useless endeavour, but still the scream.

It is the madness that sends them scampering
To underground places to inspect cuts, scratches
And the deep wounds that infect their beings.

It is the madness that sends them to their knees
As if struck down by a blast or a knife or a bullet,
And all they can do is fall and roll amidst rubble.

Tonight, I shall write about madness.

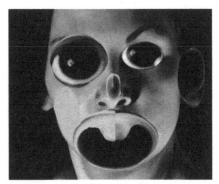

*Madness made visible from beneath the skin*

## Where Slavic Brothers Meet

Let us meet at midnight at St Peter's Gate
And step into a new tomorrow, together.

I held my enemy's hand, and through
The mangled iron, unmanned, we walked.

We had been together, face to face
Bleeding, spitting in each other's eyes.

We are together now,
                    As,
In the quiet dust-curtained yards of rubble
Our mothers hang out limp sheets and bandage.

By the twisted door to the shelter, amidst skeletons
Of dried fish and vodka, our fathers play chess.

Passing through the trampled gate, we removed
Each other's wrappings and hung them on spikes.

And, as the pawns slip forward against the clock,
We, side-by-side, are asked to rebuild Heaven.

## Inside the Basement Shelter - Donetsk

Dust falls from a shaking ceiling.
Babies cry, and babushkas shrug shoulders
And start to sing
One of those old Slavic songs.
It starts with a drone,
And moves to deep throated drawn-out notes,
Pulled from fearful throats,
Scales up and down and round,
Turning agonies of love and despair and
Drawing them in the dusty air.
The Formica table jigs a traditional dance,
Watched by a bulging eye, and steadied by veined hand,
That knows the score, It has been here before.
The newspaper wrapping unfolds and curls,
To reveal dark brown bread, black bread
The colour of soil, rich, fertile ground for grain.
Another unfolds chunks of salo, sliced thin
By the butcher's wife's simple cut with a sharp knife.
Sprinkled with salt, lemon and a wedge of garlic.
It will keep the devil away, the neighbours say.
Chess players slap the clock against time's drag
And a bottle is pulled from a baggy-loose shopping bag.
"Horilka," he breathes, he sighs
"Samagon," and they toast
"Za ná-shoo dróo-zhboo" – to friendship
"Budmo" – may we live forever.
                        And dust falls from the shaking ceiling.

## Dinner in the Hydro Park, Kyiv, 2014

(Wipe away language (yazyk in Russian) and you wipe
away thought)

The chill shiver of war is on the breeze, a tremor
Carried down the Dnipro, beyond the lights.
Tension, like a bubble's skin about to burst.

We walked home acknowledging the fears,
Fighting them with the good time memories
Just explored. And lost in the river's current.

The freak-show fairground frozen in a dim light
Casting dangerous shadows around the edges
Of overgrown pathways.

We had grouped around a long table by the river,
Staring at the menu of limited options.
Her with the frizzy hair,
He the writer,
She the French UN translator,
He the film cameraman, retired,
She the intellect,
And somewhere inside was me.

Mixed talk in English, Russian, Ukrainian,
A stumbled French, the tongues lacking fire,
Lacking sting, burn and anger.

Yazyk was left stammering,
Simmering in the pan of avoidance,
Puttering alongside the fears of waking not knowing
What you wake into.

I stepped from the table and onto the sliding sands.
I imagined radioactive silt seeping into the river bed.
I watched the full moon take shape in the sky.
Its silver watery pathway cut by a boat.
I watched lazy metro trains head underground, leaving
The bridge whose lights gave green glow to ripples.
I sucked in the saxophone-lifted warm breeze,

Playing off the river, playing off each other.
Skinny dippers in the moonlight. Always polite,
Averting eyes, men to the left, women right.

The Ukrainian writer's brother was living in Moscow,
Working for the army. He had worked in the US,
Knew about shared weaponry, shared technology.

I heard how UN translators traded whispered slurs,
Squabbled and bickered about homeland rivalries,
As their voices discussed the war in high places.

I moved, with a sigh, like the lap of water at the edge.
I remembered the painting of soldiers
Crossing in silence on low wooden boats,

Blasted from the water by German guns.
I looked at the far bank, the golden domed Lavra.
I looked into the saints' caves of preserved truths.
I looked at the far bank, the silver toned mother,
Whose base exposes the war-souls forgotten.

With her sword and her shield,
She, Tin Tits, the Motherland statue,
Stands facing Russia.
Once with love,
Now with confusion.
Betrayed by her lover.
Betrayed by her children.

The river bond, a family fairy tale that drowned.

Where will it all end? Will it ever?
The eyes of an answer pass round the table,
To hang in a hollow socket inside a ghost-skull.

We have to live the best we can, the table said.

We paid, stood and walked through the fair,
Following the noise of conflicting karaoke,
Stepping over dust dancing drunks,
Moving round the couples kissing,
Avoiding the pulled apart fighters
Who stole drinks and traded insults.

The comrades' bloated bodies rise,
Float by on the current to the Black Sea.

"Peace, Land, Bread." Ilyich, you promised it with your name.
And the Dnipro is also Elyu-Ene.

## Natasha

Natasha, with sparkling water-blue eyes.
Natasha, with the candyfloss hair.
Natasha, with the kindest soul.
Natasha, with the helping heart.

She told me of when the 48 died,
Soldiers in a plane, shot down.
She told me how she wanted
To pick up a gun and shoot.

Me, angry.
      Me, upset.
            Me, disbelieving.
Natasha, is this you?
With head slowly nodding, she said
Yes, yes it is.

Natasha, with sparkling water-blue eyes
Full of tears. Natalka, Meni duzhe shkoda,
shcho tak stalosya. I know you brother is
A soldier, here, in your *Ukray*ina.

## Tonya's Mum

Tonya's mum is eighty.
She lives on a crossroads,
Tucked in a corner
Where borderlines meet.

Tonya came from Ukraine.
She lives in East Croydon.
She teaches Russian to diplomats.
Tonya's just been to see her mum.
In a year she plans to return home.

Tonya says she needs to support her mum.

Tonya's mum is not well.
She lives in a village
Where cellars are stocked
With food and blankets.

Tonya's mum lives in the country.
From her window she sees tractors
Used by the old collective farm.
Tomorrow she expects to see a tank.

Tonya's mum says she knows what they look like.

### Walking with Camels: Love

Let's talk about love. To do so, I need the protection of my camels. Luckily, I am told by those who listen to the breeze blowing whispers across the semi-arid land, that my camels are close by. When I go off in my camel trance, I load them up with my baggage. They are perfect for seeing and helping make sense of things. Camels have three eye lids and two sets of lashes that keep the sand out.

Their thick lips mean they can eat needles, the kind no other animal would or could touch. They can drink up to 30 gallons of water. Thick body pads mean they can lay on hot sand and not suffer. They can close their noses in a sandstorm. Camel fat makes up the hump which metabolises into water. They easily travel non-stop like the ships in the desert they are known to be. They are a source of strength and survival. They are ideal protectors when it comes to love.

Camel milk has been described to me as a Somali Viagra. But I have a strong distaste for camel milk. It left me lying momentarily impotent and feeling like I was dying in a dark, fly-ridden hotel, with guts on fire, sweat, hallucinations and extreme flux. That draining exhaustion of the shits is a foul memory. The toilet nearest to my top floor room where I lay on a creaking bed, was a mess. It emptied into the gap between the inner and outer wall, a space filled

45

with piss and shit, to which I had no option but to add. But for some, camel milk is the most important nutrient these beasts can provide. So, I keep it in mind for the dilemma of love.

> You call yourself a free spirit, a "wild thing," and you're terrified somebody's gonna stick you in a cage. Well baby, you're already in that cage. You built it yourself. And it's not bounded in the west by Tulip, Texas, or in the east by Somali-land. It's wherever you go. Because no matter where you run, you just end up running into yourself. — Truman Capote

Love has brought me unbeatable joy. In my gathering of the years, the children and the grandchildren, I count myself lucky in love. But there have been times when love has promised me one thing with the right hand and passed me a cup of camel milk with the left. I have said sad goodbyes to three marriages, a son from each. But now, as I enjoy my fourth marriage and a young daughter, I say, hand on heart, it is not all doom and gloom. It is joy!

But do not expect to make sense of it all when journeying with camels inside your imagination. Sometimes love works and sometimes, well is there anyone out there who has never experienced a broken heart or two.

"There is bound to be someone driven mad by love who will give you the chance one of these days." So wrote Gabriel García Márquez in "Love in the Time of Cholera". About forty pages in, he also writes of toilet sensations: "But first he enjoyed the immediate pleasure of smelling a secret garden in his urine that had been purified by lukewarm asparagus."

Looking at the internet, the smell of asparagus in urine seems to raise a lot of concerns. For me though this is a great description of a basic act seldom talked about in a book. Love is also a basic act made complicated by too much discussion in books, films, social media... oh the list goes on.

Peeing is a great relief when you finally find public toilets that don't cost you change you don't have, and you can let it go and flow. Love is the same. It is wonderful to find love, and to let it flow. However, love can smell rotten if you allow your nostrils to be guided only by the sulphurous by-product of asparagus. On the other hand, a good love experience can smell like a garden after a pleasing golden rainfall.

Meet my wife. Rengin. Her name means colourful in Turkish. And she is. We met on a hostile environment course where we learnt how to get out of minefields, deliver battlefield medicine, deal with kidnap and false checkpoints. In my case, cart before horse, and all that. Camels, listen to me. She gave me the kiss of life.

Sometimes, when you feel you should be dead, that stimulus is exactly what you need. For us, that kiss of life led to a daughter. I already have three sons and two grandchildren. In turn, that led to a new identity crisis and a new war, this time with those who work on check-outs in supermarkets. With it comes the occasional skirmish with the chatty one in the playground, or smiley person in the queue at the ice-cream stall.

"Oh, it is so nice to see grandad out and about. Isn't she lovely. You must be very proud."

How I enjoy the retreating red faces when I, now in my sixties, say: "Actually, I am her father." Which reminds me of Leonard Cohen's Tower of Song:

*Well, my friends are gone and my hair is grey*
*I ache in the places where I used to play*

I don't know why. I guess I am at an age where it becomes a song I relate to. And after three previous marriages, I can go with the line:

*We'll never, we'll never have to lose it again*

Love has given me fond memories, and today it brings me joy. As for the broken hearts, well for those with sadness, I am sorry. For those with bitterness: don't waste time sticking pins in that voodoo doll, it doesn't even look like me. I sang this song to the camels. It meant little to them.

*There is a fish who swims the rivers. As he swims, he steals secrets from those walking the riverbanks. He turns them into stories for princesses who want to hear about love.*

## Whisper

Shall I whisper words of Love?
Oh no, I dare not

For I would lose control
As lips part

And instead, would shout Love
From the highest point

That pierces the space between
Earthly realities

But why not, why not shout Love?
And, like a hooligan

Storm the palace of prudery
With fire.

But perhaps my love is modest.
As I shout

She may shrink to crinkles
And whisper

"Silence love, just hold me.
It is all the demonstration I need."

**Step Out (on the cliff tops in Scarborough)**

A rising wind blows along the cliffs
As gulls ride other gulls' slipstreams.
I stand watching, with thoughts
Of flight and fancy in my head, dreaming

You are on board that distant ship
Following the horizon, and, with one step,
I could plant my feet onto the deck
And find your arms to steady me.

There are no black rocks or foaming sea,
There is no drop to risk or pregnant cloud
Of heavy rain, just a step across imagination
To join in kisses, you with me, together.

## The Kindest Breeze (upon landing in Libya)

The kindest breeze
Is the one that lives
In that human space
Between desert and sea.

It is the breeze
That slides beneath
The collar, works
Around the shirt

Cools the skin
And wipes the damp
Sweat that creeps
Down the aching back.

Dare I call this love,
When your face
Fills the sky and
Blows me kisses.

## Salt

Shall we make a circle of salt
And, within the safety of its circumference,
Dance a wild Polka.

Shall we step, one, two, three
In some dreamland of abandonment,
To kick salt-walls to the wind.

Shall we swirl Raki slowly in the glass
To watch it turn through ice
White fluorescent

To light some strange tangled woodland path
That twists its way to the brain,
Turning Autumn.

Let us dip damp fingertips into the pot of salt
And embrace them with each other's lips.
The essence of salt never changes.

## Snow

It was the story of snow
That filled the spaces
Between high rise blocks,

A story of light in darkness
Where crystal caves glint,
Turned from mine-crafted tunnels

Weaving hard-packed walls
Where small girls walk
In dreams of unseen escape.

Here was the wonderland
Where fear and dark shadows
Were sucked away down chutes

To disappear into the coldness
Of frozen vaults, their ice-doors
Clang shut trap sprung and locked.

Here a mind could walk free
Unseen and naked with feet
Burning on the winding path,

Hands sticking to the walls
To be pulled with a suck of skin

As smooth fine hairs erect
Along muscle thin arms and legs in
Scrawny step carrying pubescent promise
Of a life yet to come, come it will.

Blood will spill but not here in the tunnel
Not in the running space of mirrors
Not in the place of invisibility.

As the story words stepped out
Of the ninth-floor window
You promised this world to me.

And I, in this wondrous chill,
Watched the promise as it
Floated like a magic trick

From hand to age and frame,
A story told, then written,
Then trapped behind glass,
Hung in a corridor, along
A wallpapered wall, space
Claimed in another man's hall.

*Love is delicate and can get blown away.*

## Walking with Camels: Goodbye Old Life

I have been out walking with the camels this morning.
After a few hours of trekking, we paused. Off-loaded baggage.
I hobbled them under a sun-pinked rock, lit a fire.
I borrowed a flame from the sun to warm this place of shade.
I brewed coffee and filled the space with its smell.
I stared into the flames looking for a story to tell.

It came to my eye, the picture of you dancing.
It was that dance where you put your hands on head,
You raise your knees and sway with the rhythm.
I had not seen you dance like that for years.
I was glad that you could still do it before me.
I spoke into the fire that flared with confused voices.

As I spoke, I prayed my words would reach you.
"I am sorry you feel such distrust towards me".
"I am sorry you feel I have let you down".
"I am sorry for the pain of coldness inside the heat".
"I am sorry I have failed inside this marriage."
The camels are restless with their rope-hobbles.

They sense rain in the air as they graze on thin bushes.
Don't they realise it will give them water to drink?
Fresh shoots to eat. They fear the desert moment
Of a change that needs time to grow into place.
I must loosen their ties and guide them.

*Shush! I am looking at you...*

## Buttoned up Freedom

He owned a dinner suit
But never wore it,
Opportunities never arose.

Others wore fur coats
Made from rare mammals,
But hers was made of feathers.

Beneath it
She was naked
But kept all a secret,

Whereas he was a fan
Of paint splattered dungarees
Comfortable for sailing barges.

At nights they talk
Of casting off,
Standing nude beneath the stars.

But they are like others,
Like me,
Who struggle with the buttons

That twist in their holes,
That hang in their loops,
That untwine to burst free,
That fall, roll and
Disappear into some eternity.

They could not bring
Their bodies together
With open senses,
To listen beyond the folds.

**Walking with Camels: "The patronising disposition of unaccountable power"**

My wife is upstairs recording a podcast on Turkey's Soma mining disaster, where the families of those killed continue to suffer and suffer more because of a lack of public recognition and the power brokers denial of responsibility.

More than 300 miners died after being trapped, the main cause of death being carbon monoxide poisoning. Many questions have been raised over breathing apparatus used by the miners.

It happened in 2014. Reuters reported: The deaths were caused by a fire that swept through the mine in the town of Soma, 480 km (300 miles) south of Istanbul. It was Turkey's worst industrial disaster and the world's biggest mining disaster this century.

Critics said the accident, which triggered protests, showed the government was too close to industry bosses and was insensitive. Turkey's President, Tayyip Erdogan, was prime minister at the time. He described the disaster as part of the mining profession's "destiny."

Mine operator Soma Holding denied negligence, while the government said existing mining safety regulations were sound.

Seventy two people died during the fire at Grenfell Tower, London, in 2017. Admissions of guilt have been seen as inadequate. Families living in blocks of flats with similar fire risks faced a lack of government commitment to fund safety improvements. Many fearful tenants and flat owners complained about delays and costs, worried that what happened at Grenfell Tower could be repeated.

Guardian columnist Kenan Malik wrote on May 2, 2021: The government's obstinacy is unfathomable. It is also unsurprising. For, as the Grenfell Tower inquiry has exposed, the state – at local and national level – has continually colluded with business to the detriment of ordinary people. Private companies continued to sell materials they knew could kill. Governments and regulators refused to act. Locals who spoke up were damned as "troublemakers".

The story's strapline said: "The inquiry is revealing how crony capitalism was central to the causes of the tragedy"

Almost 40 people died during the Heysel football stadium disaster in 1985, when fans found themselves crushed against a collapsing wall. Around 600 were injured. Liverpool was playing Juventus in the European Cup final. Fans were blamed for what happened. But a subsequent report on the state of the 55-year-old stadium in Belgium, showed it to be in an "appalling" condition. The report, by a senior British Fire Brigade official, was never used in any inquiry.

On April 15, 1989, an FA cup semi-final match was being held at the Hillsborough stadium in Sheffield, between Liverpool and Nottingham Forest. The crowd crush there led to 96 people being killed and 766 injured. On 1 November 2017, the Right Reverend James Jones' report, commissioned by the UK's Home Office, was published. It was titled *The patronising disposition of unaccountable power: A report to ensure that the pain and suffering of the Hillsborough families is not repeated*. It was a 30-year battle before the 96 dead were declared as having been unlawfully killed.

Efforts to avoid responsibility cast black shadows over countries claiming to be open and free. Affected people, the families of victims, are left to protest, staging rallies and letter writing campaigns. But, as in the cases mentioned above, they feel unheard or under-served by the system.

As the "bodies pile high", questions need to be asked of governing systems that move away from sympathy for loss of life, especially in tragic circumstances.

These cracks are found in the running of systems that are meant to protect people. Instead, reputation and power-brokers are put above all else. The building industry, the police, mine owners, politicians, seem to be stuck in self-protection rather than supporting people. It is an extension of the same attitude that existed during the industrial revolution that spread across the globe. Us and them. Rich and poor. The continuation of colonial attitudes, despite the fall of empires. Perhaps there is a fear that capitalism may be exposed as evil.

National leaders throughout history wanted to be seen as the identity of their nation. This need spreads to the followers, to the dissatisfied and intolerant who blame "the other" rather than see fault in nation or leader. Identity is divisive and leads to "othering"- where those who believe they represent the social norm presses their forefingers in the chests of those they see as coming from a subordinate class. This is nationalism. This is the blame game.

It walks hand in hand with a growth of hard, right wing activity across Europe and beyond. This has grown in part because of a lack of alternative voice, the expected source of which is the left.

In 2021, critics in Britain have pointed to the manifest desire to stifle protest, plus the sleaze of unchallenged spending and the dismantling of services vital for peoples' well-being. All this is denied by the UK's Government. It raises question marks over democracy. These were amplified by the Trump years and on-going pressure of the right in the U.S.

The BBC reported in November 2019: Nationalism has always been a feature across Europe's political spectrum but there has been a recent boom in voter support for right-wing and populist parties.

The common factor in the BBC report is immigration and what I would call an irrational fear of refugees and people coming to take jobs and use services. It is a fear that goes back years and highlights a failure to recognise humanity or to learn lessons.

Another shadow cast is the growth of the road to power being mapped by the cult of personality leadership. Through this they seek to by-pass democracy and bulldoze their way to the top. It is not new, but repetition suggests strong chains of control or a failure to learn lessons from the past.

Look around the world and see how many cult leaders exist, with their power base cemented by placing sons, sons-in-law, daughters, friends, cronies, in positions of influence. Take the Trump family for example. But such practice goes much wider around the globe. Leaders believe they are right and opposition is wrong. You see these people in positions of power. You may see them as fathers. Or, you may meet them in a bar, a tea shop or on the factory floor. Roman playwright, Terence, believed there is nothing in the world so unfair as a man who *thinks nothing is done right except what he is doing himself.*

Underpinning these power-driven sores on the face of democracy is the lack of opposition, especially from the voter whose allegiance has shifted from a belief in a political philosophy to one that protects their individual back yard. There is a tipping point that controlling personalities keep in balance, like standing in the middle of a playground see-saw. Keep the masses just comfortable enough so they won't join the voice of dissatisfaction.

Martin Luther King said: "Freedom is never voluntarily given by the oppressor; it must be demanded by the oppressed." But that demand is not there, quelled by apathy and if we get what we need for our daily life, why should we risk it.

What nationalism creates is not the chance to seek solutions but to kick off the blame game.

We become the sheep of powerful figures. They manipulate our fear of *the others* and demonstrate their ability and influence to protect us, our country, our identity. To make someone powerful you just need to say yes to them and accept their condescending response.

"It is the position of power itself that makes men arrogant, narcissistic, egocentric, oversexed, paranoid, despotic, and craving even more power, though there are exceptions to this rule." So says Dutch socio-biologist Johan van der Dennen. Henry Kissinger described power as a great aphrodisiac.

Perhaps it is a president, a prime minister, a high-profile businessman in the entertainment industry, the head of a large international monetary organisation. I will let you find your own answers. I wonder where Margaret Thatcher would fit into this scenario.

One of her most iconic moments in the 1980s was her "Walk in the Wilderness." Teesside Live looked back on her visit. It reported: "The then Prime Ministers was caught on camera walking across the derelict site of former steel foundry Head Wrightson, which closed in 1984.

"This divisive image is recognised by some as representative of the impact that Thatcher's economic vision had on industry and in the North-east," reported Teesside Live.

I was part of a team of reporters who covered that visit. For a start, she was not caught on camera. She was photographed during what was a staged event as part of her promise to revitalise Teesside, part of the North-East of England which had seen the closure of its steelworks, ship-building and coal mining industries. Teesside faced massive unemployment and economic decline for years. As Chris Rea, the rock star from Middlesbrough, sang of the people who lived there:

*They were born and raised to serve their steel mother.*
*It was all they taught and all they ever knew.*
*And they believed she would keep their children,*
*Even though not a single word was true.*

So we said goodbye to Steel river, Rea's name for the River Tees.

Thatcher's tough line, almost dictatorial approach, showed little care for people and their livelihoods as she took on the miners. She was prepared to tolerate the damage to communities and individuals, leaving villages and towns within the geographic areas defined by mining with little hope for the future. Within a short space of time, what were revered as jobs for life were gone. As it was in the steel industry and ship building.

In 1985 Thatcher declared victory. At the time of the miners' strike the state-owned coal industry employed a total of 221,000 people, of which 171,000 were miners working in 171 pits. By March 2005, the privatised coal industry employed fewer than 7000 people. In the UK in 2019, four deep mines remained, and 9 open cast pits were operating.

Within 10 years after the strike, 90 per cent of the workforce was gone, according to a report produced for Centre for Regional Economic and Social Research, Sheffield Hallam University.

When industry returned, it did little to help those who had suffered. An example was in former Labour Prime Minister, Tony Blair's constituency. Sedgefield, another North-East area that suffered decline.

A high -tech Japanese company making microchips was lauded as one of the saviours of Sedgefield. It attracted a lot of jobs. But for the ex-miners, it offered little. Their hands were thick, big and calloused. Such hands and fingers were not suited to intricate work involving micro-chips.

Sedgefield became home to NETPark, an £85 million science, engineering and technology site. When I checked in June 2021, it was said to have provided 450 highly skilled jobs and more than 35 companies. Sedgefield's new Hitachi factory created 750 new jobs.

Unemployment statistics are hard to find in 2021. Government no longer publishes them following the introduction of the Universal Credit scheme, for people on low incomes. Looking at the "Ilivehere" website for Sedgefield, it says the rate of unemployment is "higher than the national average, suggesting that finding a job in this area maybe hard. The rate of claiming any benefit (which includes in-work benefits) is more than 25% higher in Sedgefield than the national average, suggesting that many people maybe under employed or on a low salary."

On one hand we see slick promotion of the area as a place of opportunity. On the other, we see a higher rate of those who are missing out, who don't fit the changing profile and therefore lack opportunity. When I put this to the camels when out walking one day, one said: "But that is everywhere, it is part of life." And on she trudged, leaving heavy footprints in the mud. Another came up behind me with a nudge, as if to say, come on, we must keep on walking. I keep on walking, but my head is down.

Those who proclaim themselves great leaders and stand on wasteland, ride-a-top tanks, ride horses without wearing a shirt, create opportunities to look good, they do not last for ever. When Margaret Thatcher died some mourned, others danced around singing "The wicked witch is dead." The legacy left by these leaders is often damage that needs fixing. But always in power, I have noticed, their disciples live on and promote their cause.

Jewish Orthodox Rabbi, Meir Kahane, who was assassinated in 1990, was hated by some, adored by others There are strong examples of the Israeli Knesset trying to keep him in check. But his philosophy, I would argue, remains strong and influential in Israel, and his beliefs could still be seen guiding decision makers more than 30 years after his death.

As reported on Wikipedia: "He warned of the danger of non-Jewish citizens becoming a majority and voting against the Jewish character of the state: "The question is as follows: if the Arabs settle among us and make enough children to become a majority, will Israel continue to be a Jewish state? Do we have to accept that the Arab majority will decide?""

He added: "For me, that's cut and dried: There's no question of setting up democracy in Israel, because democracy means equal rights for all, irrespective of racial or religious origins."

Having visited behind the walls surrounding West Bank and Gaza on a number of occasions, I have seen the effects of this philosophy. I was questioned by Israeli guards when coming out of Nablus. They kept me for half an hour talking about the Queen of England and her gambling habits as she enjoyed a flutter on the horses. It was a light, controlling, conversational way of telling me who was in control.

When walking with camels, these issues, would send me round in circles. This confusion created in the different worlds I lived in and stepped between. Miners dying over here, nothing being done over there, injustice here, livelihoods crushed over there... photo-opportunity time. Suddenly they all felt part of the same world, an overload of the same thing happening and repeating. I was insignificant and remain so.

That means, of course, it is time to pick up on walking with the camels, pray I get lost and enjoy the smell of flowers.

That does not mean everything is coming up roses.

## Mass Flowering of Amorphophallus Titanum

The stench of death comes
With this giant misshapen penis
Whose glory is stared upon,
Whose emanation has onlookers
Retching into handkerchiefs.

But still they look, stare even
At rare beauty that shares
In the night its foetid fragrance.
A cheesy sweat erupts from
Deep within its flowering spasm.

It warms to human levels,
Inspired by fire or cycle of the moon,
Erect, proud, stands the cock
Before its flower crumbles to dust,
Within the hot-house cathedrals.

The undertaker bird closes its wings
And sits, hunched in black, dust coated,
Above the spectacle, eyeing it up
And down in useless waiting. It is the smell
That brings it here on carrion look out.

Mother Nature whispers the sounds
Of death's decomposing form.
The rot spares us not
From the alluring fascinations.
Do not let the beauty fool you.

## Indonesia – Sumatra

As a point of reference, I came across the *Amorphophallus titanum* in Sumatra, Indonesia. It is a plant native to the island. I, and my colleague were deported as we trained journalists around Indonesia in how to report elections. We came down to breakfast and found 30 plain-clothed police officers demanding our passports. It was before the century turned, and I remember meeting with a participant who told me how amidst the political tensions of the not distant past, a relative's head – an opposition figure – was returned to the family in a hat box. I have never been able to look inside a hat box since

## De-activating the activists

Some advice for despotic leaders
Who, from the windows of their palaces
See those who rant against them
Sleeping in tents on cold nights,
Occupying central squares, blocking
The gates to their banks and mansions.

First, open your curtains in the morning,
They may have gone away so you need to do
Nothing. But,

If you see them in a crowded space,
Consider snipers on the roof tops.
You may not need to use them, bad
For publicity, and raises concern
In the courts of human rights. But hey,
When has that bothered you.

You may not need to fire the guns, of course,
But you can scare them with trainer jets
Bought from some arms dealer, the noise,
The fear it must generate. Ha, pregnant women
Will drop their babies on the spot!

So, second, create the fear of jail, or
A beating, a shooting, buy your judges,

They will help.
Pick on the students occupying their lecture rooms.
Throw in the tear gas, make some noise, storm the place.
Tell their parents that a good spanking is needed.
Give authority to the men who like to beat their wives,
Their children. They will support you, and there are plenty.

And third, disaffirm the bad ones, and if you have
A parent who is worried, get him, or her, sacked.
Tip the scales of justice.

Make a bonfire of books. Burn them in sight of those
Who camp in the snow and ice. They will be envious
Of the warmth perhaps, perhaps not. But the books
Will burn brightly. Cross out the words that offend,
Not them, but you. Don't bother reading those books.

Turn a spotlight on the foreigners who seek refuge,
Perhaps a job, or even a place of safety for their families.
Blame them for stealing the bread from your people's plate.
Blame them for taking hospital beds. Make them pay.
Encourage the black shirts to beat them, it is okay.
So, fourth, isolate the chatter, the spread of word,
Close down social media, but not totally. A little breath
Is needed to make them feel they have a little voice.

Yes, yes, yes, give them, space to speak so the liberals
Feel they can speak. There is no need to listen, and,

It makes them feel effective for a moment. A salve for
The conscience of the bleeding hearts who can then say,
"We did something." It will never be enough to change.

Close down the newspapers, the television stations, the
Radio chatter. Make sure your strong voice is heard
On your state-controlled station. Send in the censors.
Attack the advertiser so media dwindles: a sideways
Swipe. Yes, threaten the money, their chance to be rich.

Let that be the fifth for now. You can do more. More.
Concentration camps work well. Create the face of
democracy,
You can still rig the votes.

And, if the outside world looks like it could object,
Set up a business deal that you can win, they can win. Let
Them call you democratic, see you as a useful ally. They
Will not want to damage their prospects of being powerful.
After all, you know their needs, the tricks of trade.

Close the curtains in your palace. Check for bombs under
The bed where your wife sleeps, and the bed where your
Mistress sleeps, where your children sleep. Just in case
An activist lives who does not de-activate. Just in case.
Seal off all windows and doors to the draught of fear.

I meant to ask, do you have an exit strategy? Best not to
Talk about it. Keep it in a brown envelope, in your pocket,

73

The one nearest to your heart: an organ that beats, sends
Life around your body. Look after yourself. Exercise
perhaps.
But know, while it beats, the activist has hope.

The activist has hope.
One day that heart will stop.
Sleep well.

## Trust

Should you turn to the Sun, my friends,
Remember to shield your eyes.
And protect your skin,
For the Sun cannot be trusted,
Especially in these days. And when
She hides at night,
Do you know where she is,
And who she is talking to about what?
She may well be talking about you, friend,
She may have marked you,
Selected you, pointed you out to those
Who stand under sun-shades.
That is why rebellious types, like you, friend,
Should only meet at night.
But be aware of yourself.
Behind the Moon's pale face there is a dark side.
That pale face is due to the Sun,
But at least the Moon will warn you where the Sun is.
For you who wish to remain even more heliotropic,
Be even more cautious than the rebel.
There are many false suns out there,
All hoping to rule the sky in all its turns of time.

**Parked near my apartment in Kyiv was a lorry loaded with steel security doors**

Fear does not stalk the streets,
Stand lurking in shadows or
Caught holding a newspaper
Under some yellow-fuzzy light
Casting shadows on cobbles.

No.

Fear is inbuilt to all around,
To the way we think, even
To that simple way we sound.
Fear is a part of our walking,
Our talking and our isolation.

Yes.

The money men play on it,
Without even knowing it,
With their playground brains,
Their naïve simplicity that
Is governed by fists and kicks.

Maybe.

Indeed maybe, the advertisers
Play their simplicities with fear.

An advert on the side of a lorry:
"Steel doors for your home".
Clockwork Orange ticks and tocks.

The UN had run a documentary competition around HIV and Aids in Russia. I was asked to explain to a TV company in Kaliningrad why its entry did not win.

Just before 9 pm, when kids' cartoons traditionally start before bed, the station aired its programme on HIV infected mothers aborting their babies. The film crew, without the mother's permission, filmed the abortion on a baby of 25-week gestation. Viewers, should they still be looking at this stage, could see the baby moving on the floor after it was removed from the mother. I asked the reporter what she felt about the documentary. She replied: "I can't say, I couldn't watch it." Halfway through the documentary there was an advertising break. It included a clip from Clockwork Orange, where a home is broken into and a woman raped. The advert said: Buy our security doors or this could happen to you. Later, I saw a lorry load of doors near my home in Kyiv.

Just to add: My second son Tom was born at 25-week gestation and, although it was touch and go in those early days, he lives a good life.

*The sound of breaking glass*

**Fetzen dramaturgie - when police in Kyiv pulled books off shop shelves**

I thought I was looking at you
Studiously with my new eyes,
But I found my eyes were rheumy.

I was staring at you with old eyes,
Still admiring the beauty of onion domes
But black earth showed no green shoots.

Flat land, borderland, even no-man's-land
Laying between the grip of giants,
I read your history in formatted disorder.

Fetzen dramaturgie, as broken mirrors
Smashed around my feet, every splinter
Reflects the same old story,
                   The same old story
                     The same old story of Madness!

## Sehnsucht

I came to your door,
My plastic shopping bag
Stuffed with clothes:
Underwear, a shirt, odd socks.

You spoke to me
As I stood in the rain,
On your doorstep.
Welcome signs lit up,

But your eyes shifted.
I asked if you remembered
When I met you in East Jerusalem.
You nodded, as if I had not
Showed you the route
To the Holy Sepulchre.

I asked if you had kept
The nutmeg I brought you.
I know it was little,
But you had laughed
When my right hand
pressed it in your left palm.

I served you coffee
Cooked in a pot on the stove,

Offered you my cushion
And my last cigarette.

The nutmeg had grown from
The Myristica tree, I said,
Planted for my father
After he died in Deir Yassin.

You asked where I was going.
I said I had wanted to go
To America, my dream, remember?
Were you listening? You said,

"Well, have a good journey,"
And slowly closed the door.
As it shut, I heard the click
Of the security lock.

As I walked away,
Edging by the bricks
In your neat garden,
I thought of lost memories

Did you keep the nutmeg?

## Memory

Stand near the top of your stairs.
Stare through the window there,

The stained-glass blue and green,
A story window, on the landing.

Ask yourself a question:

If you became a refugee,
What would you carry?

As for me, I would travel
Light.

Perhaps a memory of standing here.
Perhaps a dream of seeing it again.

**Walking with Camels: The eye of the storm**

When wind strikes, pinning clothes to body, like soaked rags, they whip around torso. Each line, bulge. captured.

Stones whip into face, stinging sharpness. Biting, like a thousand gnats that turn skin to red blotches, leaving sores and scrapes.

Sand blinds the eyes. Arm crooked to shield the un-shield-able. This is the day to pause walking with camels, and, with dry hoarse voice,

Bark a plea for them to kneel.

"Down" with grunts and groans and mournful bellow. So, they gather round and between them a shelter is formed against the blink of

The eye of the sandstorm. Castles built against shallow breathing bodies. The smell of comfort expelled between ribs. That musty smell

That has followed the years. And when the storm stops, look again at the new place. Has it changed much?

Stand up and continue walking with camels.

**Who is Dirty?**
(Crossing from Gaza into Israel -2009)

A voice looks at me
And orders me to remove my shirt.

Why, I ask the voice.
The voice speaks threat and says

In its quiet matter of fact manner:
"We can do it for you."

I shiver without need
Remove it and feed it into the machine.

The voice speaks again
And tells me, and the invisible ones,

I am clean.

A mother carrying her baby as walks through the rubble in Gaza. 2009. Her baby as she walks.

Operation Cast Lead also known in the Muslim world as the Gaza Massacre was a three-week armed conflict between Gaza Strip Palestinian paramilitary groups and the Israel Defence Forces (IDF). It began on 27 December 2008 and ended on 18 January 2009 with a unilateral ceasefire. The conflict resulted in between 1,166 and 1,417 Palestinian and 13 Israeli deaths (4 from friendly fire). A short while afterwards I went to Gaza to help a coalition of radio stations make programmes about issues they faced as a result of the conflict, including a shortage of housing, clean water, medicines, stress and the impact on the mental health of children. The conflict did not end with Operation Cast Lead.

**Going through Qalandia Checkpoint that divides Ramallah from East Jerusalem**
(Friday March 13, 2015)

If he were a true bird
　　　Then he would not be in a cage,
Not at all like
　　　We free flitting sparrows
Who dance along the razor wire.

We, the watched ones, wait in line
　　　A motley queue of old
And young
　　　And middle aged
Sharing cigarettes and tension.

So, when the old woman
          Bursts back down the line,
Swearing, cursing,
          The tension tightens, twists
Before releasing as turnstile gates clang.

There is man pressing his buttocks
          Into my stomach, and another
Man breathing in my ear.
          Shuffle with impossible dignity.
Shuffle and look at the cameras watching.

We sparrows who hop along the razor wire,
          We watch with knowing twitches.
You can hear us chirping.
          He is not a real bird,
          He is in a cage.
Not at all like us.
          He is not one of us.'

## The Waiting Room

Hard seats and creased magazines
Laid out beneath the clock.

There is a space to squeeze into
To watch the ebb and the flow

Where waves of beauty collide
With the high rollers of ugliness.

Here, in this waiting room, wait
For a name to be called, yours perhaps,

Amidst the hydraulic pumping of the
Factory floor, a space for you,

Where your past washes into your present,
But it fails to connect, fails because of interruption

And fails again because the clock hands turn
Demanding less space to remember what
Has been, or fathom what is to come.

## The 52 Hertz Whale (Gaza)

Thoughts still the wind.
Tonight, I am the loneliest of men.
I compete with the 52-Hertz whale.

I stand on a doorstep and smoke,
Inhaling the staleness that leaves
A bitter aftertaste, thinking whales.

It is the memories that stir this mood.
The man whose daughter lived
After being shot in the stomach.

She airlifted to Europe, and he
Stranded behind the boundary
That allows only smugglers in.

He was a 52-Hertz whale too.
I am lonely because I remember.
He, because he cannot forget.

*Almost invisible people ride on donkey carts through Gaza after the heavy duty 2009 Israeli incursion.*

## Prison

I scratch lines into the plaster
Of these grey walls.
I then strike them through,
Showing their passing.
They are meaningless, for the past
Does not exist.
How can it when the then is the same
As the continuing now.

I squat on my bucket in the corner.
From here I can see the whole space,
My whole kingdom laid out
And peopled by fairy tales.
From this position I think about the poets,
Whose words froze the hummingbird's wings,
Captured the faces of flowers
Turning upward towards
The sun.

I even have my own sun, it signals the moment
To scratch on the wall, and when to stop scratching.
Damned itch!
Without you I would not know
I was alive, I am alive
With nothing to show
But my imaginarium world.

## Walking with Camels: The Space Between the Viewer and the Viewed

I once worked on a photo-project which was looking at the space between the viewer and the viewed. When one person looks at another they might see and draw conclusions. But is that person in the same world as them, do they shape what they see by their prejudicial viewpoint. Do they look at eye to eye level, or do they look from an angle, a high point, or a low point. So many things can cast shadows on what we see. I have talked to my camels about this.

Of course, it is important how the one being looked at is feeling and which world they are in when seen. Ultimately, I ask the camels: does it matter how or what people see in me? Isn't it me and how I see myself that is more important? I guess some people want you to be what they want you to be, so they may leave disappointed. Parents are an example. My dad wanted me to be an engineer, have a trade, but that's not at all what I had in mind.

When asked by the school careers service what he thought I should be, he said a tool maker. When they asked me, I happened to mention two potential careers. One was acting, the other a journalist. The acting career was blown out of the water when I was 10. "No son of mine is going into acting. You'll end up poor." So, with much resistance and blame for being a difficult teenager, I managed to get into journalism training for a year, followed by two years as a junior reporter. University had been ruled out. "No son of mine..." The first story I covered when I eventually returned to Teesside to work as a reporter was "500 tool makers sacked". Not funny for them of course, but I had a wry smile.

Is it important to have a sense of belonging? I often speak to my camels about it, usually when we are in some unrecognisable place. Belonging gives shape to identity. I often feel I live in many different worlds, so I may be standing in one but trying to belong in another. Such is madness, and thank heavens for the camels, for even if lost they will help me find water so I can survive. I want to survive, though my madness causes confusion and doubt on that front. Am I alive? Am I already dead?

Some days I can be in a parochial English seaside town where the conflicts of the parish pump are important. Another day I can be in Israel trying to head into West Bank or Gaza and being quizzed about why I was in Yemen in 2011, even though all stamps for Yemen were in my second passport. I do not feel comfortable knowing that as I move between worlds, my footsteps are being tracked.

When I travel, I am a guest in a different culture. I may not share its values, but difference makes me welcome. When back in my own cultural space I am relegated to normality. It is a price you pay for a nomadic hopscotch existence.

When I walk through the desert with my beasts of burden, my so-called ships of the desert, I see loads of Maya Angelou quotes on various signposts. Here is an example. "You cannot really know where you are going until you know where you have been." I saw another signpost in the direction of George Harrison, my favourite Beatle. "If you don't know where you are going, any road will take you there."

People with nomadic tendencies probably don't care about such signposts. Travellers live like children, always in the moment. My father, when questioning this attitude of mine, told me: "You will die lonely and poor." I mentioned this to Oli, my eldest son. He replied: "Shit happens."

When I returned to live in Turkey in 2020 with my wife and daughter, I did a quick calculation. At the age of almost 64, I was about to move into my 30th home. This was based on travelling somewhere for six months or more. I also calculated that in one three-month period I slept in 32 different beds. Being in one place has been difficult for me.

Some of the beds I have slept in proved quite uncomfortable. They were usually the posh ones. I preferred the more interesting rooms. In Ethiopia my bed had a series of rough planks that turned over every time I moved. Breakfast was tied up outside my window, bleating all night. In Sierra Leone my bed was a rectangle of clay walls, filled with sand, with a plastic sheet on top. In Somalia a cot that sagged in the middle in a fly ridden room that had no windows and was pitch black.

They may sound awful, but for some reason I slept better than in any Hilton. Even the food was better. I confess though, when it was the goat's turn to be breakfast, I could not eat it.

Space is a curiosity for me, the space between me and others and how the one who looks sees the one being watched, only to find they are both looking at each other.

I wonder how many times I have got it wrong. Misjudged what is before my eyes. As they say you cannot judge a book by it cover.

In my youth my identity was a crisis. My Uncle Pete, who lived in the U.S. chased me, seeing me with long hair which he thought was a disgrace and needed cutting. Luckily my running skills were good enough and he smoked. It was that time in the U.S. that long hair was seen as anti-establishment, anti-Vietnam and mass protest movement. I would dress like a hippy. Long hair, love beads and scooped neck t-shirts with flared sleeves. My two-tone loons had bells down the outside lower leg. CND badges were my favourite accessory.

I tried to be a suede head for a while but hated the Abercrombie coat and customary umbrella. I had a jacket with a budgie collar that never stopped flapping. I felt an idiot. I was soon back to jeans and t-shirts. A friend who I met up with again later in life asked if I had ever grown up. "You still dress the same way as you did when we were 16," she said. I still listen to The Who when I want noise and rebellion in my life. I go on to watch Woodstock for Joe Cocker and others and dream it was me on that stage.

It takes me back to Steel River and the lines that ring true for me.

"In Rainy streets we'd kiss away the shivers

And hide our fear inside the latest craze."

How we look makes a big contribution to our identity. We choose to look the way we do for many reasons. I support, for example, a woman's right to wear a headscarf, especially if they are Islamic.

Bibi Watts from Philadelphia told the Huff Post: "When I think about my hijab, I see it as my crown. Not only is it a personal stamp of identity, but it gives me a sense of class and uniqueness."

She added: "I love unveiling for my husband at home and see myself as the gift he gets to unwrap each time I take my hair down. I love the feeling of having my beauty be a secret and not getting caught up worrying about the demands of society."

Yet others will question her choice as being controlled. But, as I understand it, wearing the hijab is about how you behave and treat others. But I do think it has to be a choice women make for themselves within their own cultural beliefs and connections.

And when a woman removes her headscarf, that can be a powerful moment. I learnt this when I met Edna Aadan Ismaaciil ama Adna Aadan Ismaaciil, a former Somaliland politician and international campaigner against female genital mutilation. She showed me a secret recording of an FGM operation being carried out. I saw fear in a young girl. I saw brutality in those who said they loved her. And then I was an onlooker with her at a conference, where a woman removed her headscarf.

*The viewer and the viewed*

## The Women's conference on FGM in Somalia

Together we watched as women gathered.
Men were not supposed to see, but I was allowed.
I watched from a monitor as the conference unfolded.
I watched as the stooped old woman leant on her cane.
Refusing help, she climbed the stairs.
I watched her move slowly to the microphone.
Suddenly, she became tall, aquiline and straight,
Although she barely moved. Her eyes brightened.
Emotion, it held back her voice, deep in her throat.
But then, the room fell silent. Hush, hush, they saw
What I saw. Magical movement, that quashed distance
Between her, me, and the crowd that watched.

She removed her headscarf and spoke.

"For eighty years I have been waiting
To remove my headscarf and talk about this."

## Space Between the Viewer and the Viewed

This space may be filled with rainbow-striped balloons
Floating in the freedom of thought, flaring to rise higher.

Perhaps it is within this space that the high art thoughts
Of love, romance and passion may float on a gondola.

Silver balls of great philosophy may bounce around here,
Along with the theories and chalk dust of experimentation.

It could be simple: this space between our eyes is where
The electro-magnets zip their energies to ping-zing between us.

This is the space where the Tardis sits, unmoving but waiting
For the clock to stop so a step can step in and a step can step out.

This space is soup.

This space is the vacuum where the empty bandwagon may travel
With rattle and rock at erratic speed in a tumbleweed roll.

This space is the ghost town where spirits walk through walls
Of broken histories, firing disturbant flashes from rooftop rifles.

This is the space of ambush where souls are fooled, thinking
They see through the space, but do not see through it at all.

This space is the sweating place for fantasies between the viewer and the viewed,

Where the who is looking at who but who can see what the other sees
Beyond the false mirrors of warped reflections pinned to walls.

This space is unstable isotope.

This space is where the shoulder monkey sits with his pin
Popping balloons as they fly-by, satisfying disappointment.

This space is where the fates and hates can plough their furrows
And plant their seeds to grow like mushrooms and black clouds.

This space is the blackest of holes, empty and void of emptiness,
A walk in, run through mirror-shards thrown like discus-spears.

This space is the kissing gate where a look meets the eye and the eye,
Meets the soul of another, where reaction turns and turns
again, moving into

This space,
        That has no conclusion.

*Tense Space*

## Identity

I must keep my mouth tight shut.
It holds my face up and
      If I move,
             my face will slide down
And I
Will become instantly recognisable.
I can move with this microphone
But the wire only
      Stretches so far
             And the speaker only
Goes
      So loud, it holds my voice back.
I am a mountain of contradictions,
Too many secrets
      I cannot reveal
             Or my worlds will become known
And I
      Will become an imbalanced juggler.
Danger grows sharper when the balls
Are made of thin porcelain
      So fragile
             You can see light's glimmer.
Bone China.
      They are bone some say but even thinner.

There are days when I can feel
My face slipping.
      With rubber hands
            I try to keep it in place.
I am
      Scared I will leave my fingerprints all over me.

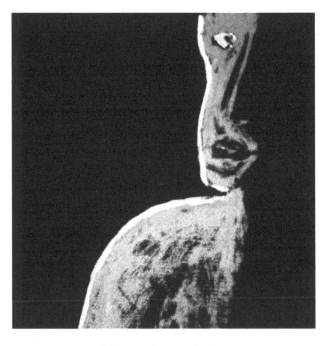

*Self portrait – a painting*

## Rainy Night outside a London pub

Cigarette, I asked.
Stopped, I replied.
Raincoat shoulders
Spattered with rain.
Hat brim filling
With falling water.
Water spilling onto
Raincoat shoulders.
Cold chill, Collar up
Feet standing in a puddle.
Shoes leaking
Through a sole hole.
like this one
Soul hole feeling
Worked with a wagging
Big toe.
Car drives through a puddle.
Cigarette, I ask.
Matches wet, I reply.

## The Drowning of Virginia Woolf

To walk in the footsteps of a memory
That was lost beyond its own horizons,
Down a muddy, cowpat splattered path.
Leaning into a wind to catch its every breath,
A word-blown soundscape snagged
On every bending tree's brittle twigs,

To be stripped back to naked honesty
As red-golden patterns swirl around, lifting
That musk-smell of fermenting leaves.
Walk, counting the stones you could retrieve
And place in your pockets; enough to carry.
Enough to weigh you down, to keep you

Down under the muddy-brown waters,
To let your flesh chill and your soul
Join the realm of fish. Here your eyes
Can, fishlike, link to the new world unknown
Within uncharted dreams and imaginations,
Unblinking visions bending weed and water.

Not once, perhaps twice, even thrice and more,
You have endured the shocks of suffering, visited
Too many *forme di vita diverse,*
                              All in one head.

Really, it is a wonder we survive the shocks.
We truly need the shelter of the past, but where,
Where can we go when the shelter of the future

Is lost?

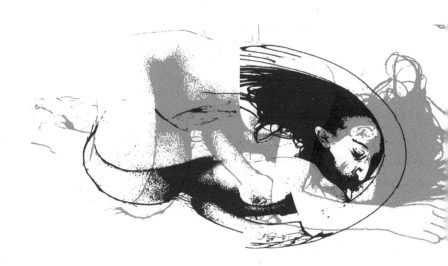

*Trapped in a closed space*

## Final Call

A woman wearing rainbow gloves
Talked long and clearly into her phone.
She did not speak to one, but to as many,
As many she hoped would listen.
                                    "Listen".
She said it in a voice of squeaking parquet,
Stepped upon by leather soles worn
By people with souls of leather and polish.
I heard her message immediately, but not
Them, those who were not present at the
Time of speaking. They would hear her later,
After her deed was complete. When the phone
Would be found in her patch pocketed coat.

Should I talk to her about bible black days,
Of love and loss, of break up and break down?
I could not match hers, or her response. Myself,
Too weak, but she, calm in her ways and deliverance.

Her choice, and her blue eyes within creased eye sockets
Looked dry, content with their goodbyes, folds
Of facial skin relaxed around her pocked nose.
Her one way ticket punched, she was in control.

I stepped off at Gatwick, ready to fly, and watched
Her pull away to Brighton where the beach has stones

## The Pike

I lowered my face to the water
And watched my reflection scatter
With a myriad of fishes darting.

The pike looked at me, long
And I whispered in his ears
As he made his rueful turn
And disappeared, with scorn.
But the fateful day arrived, and
I saw him again, airborne, flapping
Dangling from a hook. Snared
In a net, and I watched my prophecy,
Quietly shared with him, come true.

He still swims defiant within his case of glass,
Mouth open, eyes bulged, drowned within
An airless tomb, predicting in whispers to my ear,
I ponder his pathway to some place.
I ponder the power over his displaced
Sense of home, sense of space and sense of time.
I know his prediction, his coffined state,
Will one day overbear me and all
That has been claimed mine.

But I will not remain in a glass case.

## The House

I built a house
Like the one I always wanted to build,
With a clock tower.

I built a clock,
An old fashioner ticker turning hands,
And attached it

To the top
Of the clock tower's weathervane,
Shaped like a cock.

And the clock
Floated timelessly above the roof.
And I lived below.

I had a bed
With a firm feather mattress
And slept well.

I had a bath
With gold mermaid taps pouring
Hot water bubbles.

I had a table
That sat twenty for dinner and
I ate alone.

I threw a party
And everybody came, so I left
The house floating,
                    … and kept going

## Thoughts around a dinner table in a foreign land

I am bored inside my cupboard,
Despite its glass door that I peer through,
Where others can peer back.

We sink into after dinner speak.
Our language differs.
Our translators lie with smiles.

You speak with clever tongue not knowing
That being clever is no match for intelligence
And that intelligence is rusted when attached to elite.

I am a guest in your culture whereas you,
On this occasion, cannot be a guest in mine.
I am the visitor lost in a world of misapplied plenty.

Boredom in a remembered dead culture,
Buried under the heel push, buried by those
who do not look where they tread.

Talk dies in admiration,
Which, after death,
Sits in God's waiting room.

And so we converse, after dinner,
Until the eyes get tired of listening
To what the ears cannot see.

## Dignity

"Understand me.
Be with me.

Shun me if you wish.
But let me swim with dignity."

She swam,
Head held like a swan,
Through deep cool water
Of a lake lined with pines.

Beneath the breaking tension of the surface
Her arms, legs, pushed her forward,
Motion pulling her onward with grace,
Denying the chaos of her legs.

Pining eyes in the forest watched
As ripples kissed the shoreline.
And in the trees the wide-eyed owl,
The nervous woodcock,
The thieving magpie,
The silent woodpecker,
Were still.

And those who cannot swim,
And those who cannot fly
In the strange world of water,
Could not understand her words:

"Understand me.
Be with me.

Shun me if you wish.
But let me swim with dignity

Inside my own fluid madness."

## Walking with Camels: A Beetles Fan

I have seen many miraculous recoveries. In cramped, oil-smelly garages I have seen old mechanics with ancient tools cannibalize one 60-year-old Beetle to get another started. And I love it! It is like witnessing the last miracle in the Gospel of John.

I dream of Beetle. I love the egg shape and having an engine in the wrong place. I would fill her up – always she – and travel to wherever she would take me. That is not to say I would abandon my camels. As I drive, kicking up dust in the wake of my wheels turning, I would still have them with me. In my head. On holiday perhaps.

I have bravely assisted my eldest son Oli on two long distance car rallies. It is one of the best things a father and son can do together. The first was London – Mongolia. We never made it. After crashing, we relied on a Turkish mechanic with a heavy hammer to keep us going... but got turned back at the Azerbaijan border. If only we'd had a Beetle, although our fashion-box four-wheel drive car, costing 400 pounds, was fun.

The second was London to Marrakesh. A couple of mechanical faults and speeding tickets on the way, and the clutch went on the way back, leaving me stranded with bottles of wine and great cheese on a campsite in France for a week, whilst OIi hitch-hiked home. The camels had a great time with all the fresh green grass. Again, if only we'd had a Beetle, not an ancient Ford Escort.

George Harrison remains my favourite Beatle. His philosophy of life kind of goes hand in hand with the old Beetle way of living. George, bless him, believed you kept on being reincarnated until you found truth. He also said: "life on Earth is but a fleeting illusion edged between lives past and future beyond physical mortal reality."

Well, as we go through life's stages we certainly experience re-birth in a kind of one door closes, another opens type of way. I noticed my life is shaped and divided by marriages, experiences, career changes, kids born, travel times. You go through that time-in-your life, a new door opens, and you change. Sometimes you even learn from mistakes made in the previous life.

The biggest example for me was after West Africa and then East Africa, set against comfort and wealth versus poverty and conflict. It changed my life and led to radical decisions to move on. This of course coupled with a dose of yet to be identified PTSD. Since then I have kept moving on and now live in Turkey.

Turkey is the place I feel most at home. Istanbul is a classic crossroads place where the Silk Road passed, and Europe and Asia divided. It is a hub for going places in the Middle East, Asia and Africa, across the old Ottoman empire, or across the Black Sea and the spread of land where Cossacks rode.

As a child, living in Buckingham, my desire to see the world began. We were a Grattan family. All our clothes came from the Grattan catalogue, including my pyjamas. The only kind I would wear were Cossack style. At night I would play being Taras Bulba, based on the Tony Curtis Hollywood version. And I dreamed of going to the Steppes and riding ponies.

Later I studied political history, including the Soviet Union. It linked back to my fascination with Cossacks, Ukraine and Russia. I started my own Egglescliffe Sixth Form Communist Cell and wrote protest letters. It was a very small cell and to the best of my knowledge, did not raise any eyebrows or be considered any kind of security threat.

Somehow, in my early years I knew I would visit Ukraine. Back in the USSR was one of the first songs I learnt on the guitar. And I did. It was like a sixth sense, I had a feeling I would live there. It is like I had a similar feeling that Africa and I would be linked. Reading Graham Greene's The Heart of the Matter, and its link to Freetown in Sierra Leone, made me feel I wanted to see this place where heat and humidity led to weakness and pity and battles with compassion. You can sense "the smell of flowers under a balcony, the clang of corrugated iron, an ugly bird flopping from perch to perch."

In West Africa I found meaning in Greene's line that: "Nobody here could ever talk about a heaven on earth. Heaven remained rigidly in its proper place on the other side of death, and on this side flourished the injustices, the cruelties, the meanness that elsewhere people so cleverly hushed up."

This was something to mull over with the camels, the cicatrice this book left on my memory and how I matched it to the place. Later, re-reading this book, Greene summed up something I had felt, when he described how the main character, Scobie and the "ultimate border he had reached in happiness: being in darkness, alone, with the rain falling, without love or pity."

Books are dangerous. You get so drawn in that sometimes that one book, for a while, becomes the one prism you see the world through. But that quote was key to meeting up with my camels and keeping them inside my head. I saw the shape of the hole dug by PTSD, the rough edges of its deep sides.

I watched a Netflix series called Black Spot. In it the main character, Police-Major Laurène Weiss, finds herself trapped at the bottom of a chasm, her colleague, Baloo, bleeding to death by her side. She knows help is needed so tries to get out. As she nears the top of an arduous climb, she slips and falls back down. Then an ethereal stag appears and shows her the way out. I wish it was that easy. My camels don't show me the way, our conversations and walking are meant to help me discover it

Moving to Turkey, meeting my wife and having a child, helped me consolidate my climb out of the hole. I also had a feeling that one day I would live in Turkey. I had visited Istanbul many times before moving there, before I even knew my wife. I had fallen in love with the place, a complete contrast to West Africa, or Kyiv, or anywhere else. It is the ultimate crossroads where cultures meet.

Visiting and living there are very different. Living there you become part of the hustle and the bustle. You develop your coffee shop routines, your lunch stops, your hellos to market traders, your favourite fish restaurant, mehanes and raki brands, and argue the toss between EFES and Tuborg beers.

But for me, my joy was using the ferries to get out to the islands or from one side of the city to another. I loved the walk on and finding a spot on the outer decks. Watching the wake as the ferry cut across the water. Seeing the mosques and towers with a cup of Turkish tea. Drinking it on the ferry was a must do for me, whether I needed one or not.

Turkey, with its difficult politics, intrusive lifestyle,

crowds and smells and chatter and café society, was the place I felt like home. I had a similar, but not so deep feeling, when living in Belgrade, with its café society feel. For different reasons, when living in Dar es Salaam in Tanzania, much connected to outdoor lifestyle, living on the porch cooking fresh fish, and seeing wildlife.

My camels are well travelled. Every place I have been has connections with difficulty, tragedy or negativity. But at the same time, I discovered the glory and beauty of these places as well. It was a rare experience for example to find myself standing alone, silent, in Istanbul's Blue Mosque, one of my favourite places on the planet. I am not a Muslim, but this moment was spiritually enriching, captured in silence.

These places I mention as being good to live have one thing in common. There were lots of Beetles driving around, old Beetles, survivors thanks to hammers, nuts, bolts and spanners, a bit of welding perhaps.

The Beetle. I quite like two toned ones rather than the usual single colour and prefer a roll back inset sunroof rather than a fold back one. Beetles are to me what a crucifix was to Greene. You keep going by working your way forward. The difference is you don't place heaven on the other side of death. You accept this is where you are, your insignificance and the challenge to find your road. And it doesn't matter. If you don't know where you are going, you will find out when you get there.

Beetles. Where are the camels? Well, they are in my head, carrying my baggage. There is not that much space in an old Beetle which fills quickly with noise, bone-shaking vibrations, and oily smells. Read on.

## Bukashka (Russian for little beetle)

She came to life in 1967,
With her curvaceous back,
That flows into the space
Where her vibration starts.

She rattles and she rolls,
Coughs in the mornings,
And dances over potholes
As she pings and sings.

She is a fashion icon
One of a kind, today
A retro superstar,
A grand title for a car.

She is as was the classic
Rolling stone, emerging
From the dust of the day,
With rain washed streaks.

Hundreds of VW Beetles
Pound the streets of Addis,
A thousand cold war Bukashkas
Rev and thump their way.

Or grind or stomp, or flop,
And splutter to the stop,
To be stripped naked,
Helping others live another day.

I looked in at his graveyard
Of rust-bucketed beetles,
I watched as his blowtorch
Glowed red, spanner clanked.

And, as the grease spreads,
The rust glowing in piles
Upon the hard mud floor,
His voice would whisper:

                    "God give her one day more."

## The Cats of Istanbul

A thousand and more cats' eyes
Peer down from the roof tiles.
A thousand more from inside
The fish bone full waste bins
Of emptying meyhanes.

On the street, the red glowing
Tip of a cigarette arcs up and
Spirals down to the ground,
As the last swaying, imbalanced
Human, takes leave of the night,

Steps aside, leaving ashtrays full.
So, the bins fill even more with
That stale smoke smell, that
Remnant of fish head and bony spine.
The air and the hair bristles dinner.

Boundary marking piss and calls
Echo vibration around bare streets,
As the lamps turn down to a jaundiced glow
And mist rolls in from the Sea of Marmara,
As drunken sailors snore to the moon.

The lingering Prophet's fingers
Leave stripe marks on the backs
Of those moving low and fast, to
Statue-stillness in an instant, like
Assassins in the night shadows.

Shrouding Sultanahmet in the remains
Of His torn cloak, He offers them darkness
To scuttle in, freedom of the city, these
Creatures born from a lion's sneeze,
That rocked the Ark, and

Sent mice and rats running with a shiver,
Fearing for their lives, nipping the leftovers
As they move, as cats pounce, claws bare,
Pounce again to toss and play with
The prizes found amidst the garbage.

There in the cough of the morning
Lay the heads of rodents, bloodying
The doorsteps of waking cafes and bars,
Waiting for the hungover sailors return.
As a thousand or more eyes close in peace.

*Searching in the mine of madness... a solution, a cure...*
*maybe it's round the corner.*

## Haydarpaşa Train Station, Istanbul (For Rengin, Nur, Akin and Nazim Hikmet)

The eyes of my favourite colour
They stare down the lines of ruin
And grow damp.

Here memories of arrival, of leaving
Chug into platforms.

Life's bustle paused with the impatience
Of cancellation.

But no apology comes from rusting speakers
Splattered with bird shit.

No squeal, no hiss, no steam in the heart,
No clang of steel on steel.

Ruin stands by tarnished buffers where
Engines once kissed home.

*In an orderly fashion I cartwheel before her,*
*And toss a packet of cigarettes.*
*I turn, stop and stare.*
*I cartwheel back and toss towards her*
*A burning match.*
*Stop.*
>*And stare.*
*The ghosts of Haydarpaşa are here.*

*Abandoned and abused, - A train graveyard near **Haydarpaşa**, once Istanbul's link to the rest of Turkey.*

## Istanbul

Those night shadow streets
Where intrigue roams,
                The catcalls,
                                The shouts
And loud rows that explode out of windows. It's
Long yellow taxi lines and corrupted fares to
Belly dancing rhythmic hot spot traffic jam frustrations.

I stand in awe, in reverence to its blue tiled match
Of Persian, Turkic, Arab, Indic swirling mix of Dervish dance
And art and history and language rich, of blood and guts
And war and peace, of piracy and slaves and tales
Whispered by the bending reeds into the ears of story-spinners,

Retold and resold in cold war tones of plot and smuggled
Into a pocket or a pipe that bubbles and breeze that wafts
The sweet-sour scent of strong tobacco across the alleys
To swirl with the aroma of coffee cooked to predict futures
Spiced from the Egyptian market, moistened with oils and essences

Attacking nostrils that lead the nose into the grime
Of the Beyoğlu's Kasimpaşa district where sellers spit and
Chew as they trade their rattling lorry loads of pastes and purees,
Herb bushels and nuts, sack splitting and spilling grain, and amidst
This tour, like an old hypocrisy, the Sahaflar book market survives.

Stopping for mint tea, to catch the air and sounds, the jams,
Scams led by lanterns in a round-a-bout chase of kiss and tell, squealing
Voices rising, falling, tram rattling, tattling the tales of who is selling who. Oh,

The crudity of storytellers who sell the pages of prejudice and fear the censor's
Will to protect the inquisitors' realm and regime from question.

Is there hope? Parental fear, student noise, those bricks broken,
Hurled, bones breaking, secular desire versus religious fervour,
Protest in the park, tears and gas, gas and tears, sooths and seers,
The heavy hands, another battle within the streets of fleeting shadows
Thrown by fire against the flaking aged walls of narrow thoughts.

Istanbul, a notch in my collection of crossroads
Cross-stitching the world together, romantic Istanbul.
I read Ahmed Hâşim's new style,
Away from Dawn of the Future,
Traced the human landscapes of Nâzım Hikmet,
Humanity imprisoned brought tears.
Orhan Pamuk led me blindfolded through Snow.
All,
In the pages of exile and imprisonment

And me
Sitting in Taksim Square, sleep-reading in Kinross' room,
Talking to black-eyed transvestites,
rape victims,
And hushed voices of freedom in compromised tone.

I return to the Blue Mosque and I am told
If I whisper over here, the man over there
Will hear. It is still best to stay silent in Istanbul. Silence...

I smoke the silence.

Urban madness. Horn-blaring circle-pattern
Parades around the city. The setting sun paints
Blood stains on palaces along the polluted Bosporus,
And the vibrating, unsettled soul murmurs ancient intrigue,
As the azan vibrates through mist woven jumble-sprawl.

And I remember the restaurant overlooking it all, eating
Sea bass with my fingers, freshly grilled juice-seeping
Flesh. And flesh of trapped daughters given to the grey wolf;
Of the nine "Oguz" whose voices fluctuate, projected confused (reference)
Between the world stage and the silenced platforms, ears pricked.

They speak the essence of being Turkish, glorious virtues so stated
In language of the *noblesse oblige*d whose trade is rooted firmly
Within the moral economy, or the economy of morals, hauling self
From the crumpled sheets of a sick-bed, bathing in tradition and,
As in history, bending tradition to suit the circumstance of the day.

Turkey sets again her stall in this marketplace, masterfully displaying
Her table-top of gifts parked on her crossroad of power between East
And West. She squirrels her own sins to the bottom of the pile.
On the top she piles the sins of neighbours and gossips wrapped
In her bartering tongue. Sultan Hürrem strolls again amongst the peacocks
And walks beside the tulips behind the palace walls,
Those protective walls upon which those shadows dance,
On both sides, they dance and dance and dance more,
Running huge, running small and merging into one mass
Of over-shadows, clashing and melting into a riotous montage
                                                    of Istanbul.

*Away from the urban madness and into the alcoves of intrigue.*

## Walking with Camels: Ear Whispering

When walking with camels,
Shouting at these stubborn beasts
Does little good.
Whisper in their ears.
"Move along."

Whisper,
As lovers do,
A soft encouragement.

It is the shouting that makes them
Stubborn.
Shouting,
As lovers do,
Makes me stubborn too.

The art of whispering
Brings bodies and souls
Together.

Share need:
Let us find food.
Let us find water.

Into their ears:
"Move along."
And walk beside them.

## Walking with Camels: Stopping

"A good traveller has no fixed plans and is not intent on arriving." So says the "axial" sixth century philosopher from China, Lao Tzu. Well that was the way with me.

I just needed to move, and, I did, until I got to Turkey. Suddenly I found myself paused, married and once more a parent.

I never really knew where home was after more than 25 years of living and working on the road. Turkey seemed the right place to lay my pork pie hat.

In the words of George A. Moore: "A man travels the world over in search of what he needs and returns home to find it."

If I needed a cure for madness, well I probably never found it, but I am learning to manage it better.

As John Steinbeck wrote: "Many a trip continues long after movement in time and space have ceased."

So, what did happen to those camels.

## Walking with Camels: Turning Point (For Rengin and Maya)

There came a day, when I was out walking with camels,
That I stood still.

I sat down upon my stumbling block and contemplated
The walls around me.

These were the walls that kept me in and the walls that
Kept me out.

I wondered which was which and thought of tunnels
And pole vaulting.

As I considered the space above and the space below to be cleared,
The camels walked.

Their rough woollen covered ribs rubbed the walls as they
Circled, leaving musty traces.

Beneath the smears I considered graffiti writers'
protest, blindly scrawling on differing sides of a wall.

Curious was I at how they could never see each other's
Complaints, only their own.

And the eyes that watched them were the eyes of agreement,
Set in banging skulls.

I had walked through chimerical landscapes.
I had run beneath the ceilings of dried eyeless fish heads.

I had drunk camel milk
With the princes and the paupers, conversing in tongue rolling platitudes,

And shared my sickness
With the hustlers and the hookers before escaping to deserts, holding

My creased map showing where
Stars shone,
      where seas had washed
            and plates slid and shifted.

And there it was,
The world of walking in trapped geographies and altered histories.

So, I squatted, drank coffee, smoked as camel herders do,
and drew meaningless lines in dirt.

I let my camels go.

I turned my back and saw you walking towards me.
The walls lost their questioning.

### Walking with Camels: A Gift

If you see one of my camels walking freely, feel free to take it home. Your home. Wherever that may be. If you are hungry to the point of starving, eat it. Don't drink the milk, there are children waiting. Give it them. If you need a helping hand, load up the camel. Just make sure it finds water and food. Keep it nourished. Make sure you have the energy to travel with it. But be prepared to let it go when you are sane and ready.

As Confucius said: "Wherever you go, go with all your heart."